The Saints
VOL. I

Text
Louis M. Savary

Illustrations
Sheilah Beckett

Cover Illustration
Michael Letwenko

THE REGINA PRESS
New York

Mary, Queen of all Saints and Mother of Jesus, I know how much you love me. Let me come to you, Blessed Mother, to share all my joys and sorrows.

MARY, QUEEN OF SAINTS

Mary was an only child. She grew up loving God very much. Out of all women in history, God chose Mary to be the mother of His own Son, Jesus. When God's angel asked Mary if she would be the mother of Jesus, Mary answered yes.

As His mother, she was at Jesus' side when He was born in a stable in Bethlehem; she found Him when He was lost in the Temple at Jerusalem; she was with Him when He died on the cross on Calvary; and she was in the upper room to welcome Him when He rose from the dead on Easter.

In heaven, Mary was crowned Queen because she was mother of Jesus, mother of all the saints, and mother of the Church. That makes her our mother, too. Whenever we pray to Mary, we may call her mother, our Blessed Mother.

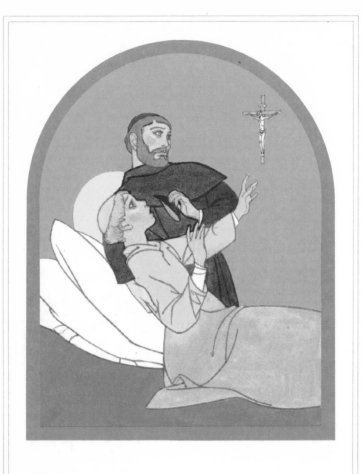

Saint Aloysius, you studied hard, helped the sick, and loved Jesus and Mary with all your heart. Help me to be like you in your kindness and love.

SAINT ALOYSIUS GONZAGA

Aloysius Gonzaga was the son of a very noble Spanish family. His family expected him to marry and become a famous nobleman. But Aloysius was not interested in getting married or becoming famous.

At a young age, Aloysius joined the Society of Jesus. Among these young men, he was outstanding for the holiness of his life. He put aside all his expensive garments and wore only the cast-off clothing of others. He was also very brave.

When a terrible plague came upon Rome, Aloysius went out to care for the sick. He even brought home a very ill old man and took care of him in his own bed. Eventually, young Aloysius became sick and died in 1591.

He wanted very much to become a priest, but he did not live long enough. He is a patron saint of boys and girls.

 aint Anne, mother of Our Lady and
grandmother of Jesus, you never stopped
praying. Help me when I feel discouraged
and need hope.

SAINT ANNE

Anne is known to us because she is mother of Mary and grandmother of Jesus. Anne and her husband Joachim loved God and prayed for a child. It seemed God did not hear their prayers because years went by and a child never came. But they kept praying.

When it seemed Anne was too old to have a child, God gave them one. They called their special child Mary, a name which means incense that rises up to God. Anne's daughter became the woman that all Jewish women longed to be, the mother of the Messiah.

Anne was proud of Jesus. As His grandmother, she often had the opportunities to hold Him and play with Him. He often came to her house to visit.

Anne, whose name means "full of grace," was a holy woman.

Saint Anthony, you were asked by God to live your life in preaching and in caring for the needy. Help me to live for God and God's people.

SAINT ANTHONY OF PADUA

Statues or paintings of Saint Anthony often show him holding the Divine Child in his arms. That is because one night the Christ Child came to visit Anthony, kissed him, and told him how much He loved him.

Anthony often prayed that he would be a martyr. Instead, God asked him to live and work among the poor and the needy.

The Franciscan Order encouraged him to travel throughout Europe preaching the story of Jesus. The power of Jesus was so evident in everything Anthony did, that miracles happened. Small amounts of food multiplied to feed many people when Anthony blessed it. People with incurable diseases became well when Anthony touched them. People flocked to him, and children loved him. Everyone cried when the church bells announced that Anthony had died in the year 1231.

Saint Augustine, you can understand how people often turn away from goodness. Help those of us who sometimes find it difficult to be good.

SAINT AUGUSTINE

Augustine's story is that of a young man who was a sinner but who, by God's grace and his mother's prayers, became a wise and holy person. Augustine's mother Monica (who is also a saint) tried to make her son change his ways. "Make my son a good man," she begged God every day.

But clever and bright Augustine preferred not to be good. He fell in with bad company and led a wicked life. He was bright enough to know that what Christ taught was the truth, but he just did not want to be good.

One day, Augustine decided to change his way of life. He became a priest and later was named a bishop. He used all his energy and intelligence to help the people of God. "Our hearts are made for You, O Lord," he once wrote, "and they are restless until they rest in You." He died in 430.

*S*aint Bernadette, you were only a little
child when Our Lady appeared to you.
Help me to find Jesus and Our Lady in
my own life.

SAINT BERNADETTE

On February 11, 1858 in Lourdes, France, Bernadette and her childhood friends went out to the fields to gather firewood. Bernadette came to a cave near a river, and saw a beautiful Lady dressed in blue and white, with stars around her head and roses at her feet.

When Bernadette told her family about the beautiful Lady, they did not believe her. But the Lady kept reappearing. One day the Lady told Bernadette to dig where she stood, and a fresh spring of water came bubbling out of the ground. Blind people who washed their faces in the spring could see. Sick people who washed their bodies in the water became well.

The Lady told Bernadette to build a great church there. This came to be known as the Shrine of Lourdes. Many miracles still happen there to this day.

Saint Catherine Laboure, you loved Our Lady so much that she used you as an instrument to make many miracles happen. Help me to pray with faith and fervor.

SAINT CATHERINE LABOURE

Catherine was born on a farm in France in 1806. Catherine walked miles each morning to attend daily Mass. Despite her father's reluctance, she became a Sister of the Daughters of Charity.

From childhood, Catherine experienced the presence of God and Our Lady in her prayer. In the convent, Our Lady appeared to her three times, telling her to have a holy medal made with the picture of Mary, the Immaculate Conception, stamped on it.

As soon as people began wearing the medal, miracles started happening. The medal soon began to be called the Miraculous Medal.

Catherine never told anyone but her confessor about the visions. So, even at her death in 1876, no one knew that Catherine was the one who brought the Miraculous Medal to the world.

Saint Dominic Savio, you found happiness in working hard to help other poor and homeless children. Show me how to be joyful in doing what I have to do.

SAINT DOMINIC SAVIO

Dominic, born in Italy in 1842, was only fifteen when he died. He had been a pupil of John Bosco, and grew up in his Home for Boys. Dominic had been a homeless child and John Bosco loved him as if he were his own son.

At an early age, Dominic organized a group of people called the Company of the Immaculate Conception to help John Bosco. Dominic's group was very poor, but they struggled together joyfully and worked hard to make the homes of John Bosco succeed.

Dominic wrote many letters to his friends about his joy in helping poor and homeless children. Dominic is a model for young people who want to do important things for God.

Saint Elizabeth Seton, you endured sadness and misunderstanding from many people. When I am sad or hurt, help me to find comfort in knowing God loves me.

SAINT ELIZABETH SETON

There was much joy in the United States in 1975, for that was the year when Elizabeth Ann Seton was declared a saint. She was the first American saint to be born in the United States, but she was not born a Catholic. She was a convert.

In New York, where she lived, she opened a boarding school for children. Her husband had died, and this was the only way she had to support herself and her children. In 1805 when Elizabeth became a Catholic, St. Peter's was the only Catholic Church in New York City.

A priest encouraged Elizabeth to move to Baltimore and open a boarding school for Catholic girls, which she did. She and the women who helped run the new school wanted to become Sisters, so they started their own congregation called the Daughters of Charity in 1809.

Saint Frances Xavier Cabrini, you always said that God did everything. Help me to trust that God cares for me and what I am trying to do.

SAINT FRANCES XAVIER CABRINI

Frances Cabrini was born in Italy, in 1850, but America claims her as a saint because she became an American citizen in 1909.

In Italy, she tried to enter several religious communities, but they all refused to accept her because her health was poor. When she began working with five other women at an orphanage in Italy, the bishop closed the orphanage. Next she asked the Pope if she and her companions could go to China as missionaries. He said no, and sent her instead to the United States. When she arrived in New York, the bishop advised her to return to Italy.

However, she remained in New York, opened orphanages and schools, and began a small hospital. She and her companions founded the Missionary Sisters of the Sacred Heart.

*S*aint Francis of Assisi, you showed us how God created all people, animals, and plants to live together in unity. Help me to love all creatures God made.

SAINT FRANCIS OF ASSISI

As a young man, Francis was very wealthy and enjoyed the pleasures of life. But once when he was sick, he felt that God was calling him to live as Jesus did. Francis responded to God's call and began to visit the sick in hospitals and to do helpful things for the poor. "When people serve the poor," Francis said, "they are serving Christ Himself."

Francis began to wear clothes like the poor, and he started to preach to people about peace and unity. Francis often addressed the sun, moon, stars, and animals as brother or sister.

Once during prayer Francis had a vision of Jesus hanging on the cross. So deep was Francis' desire to be like his Lord, that the marks of Jesus' five wounds appeared in Francis' body and remained there all his life. He died in 1226.

$\int$aint Francis de Sales, you spent your life with the words of Jesus on your lips. Help me always to use Jesus' name with reverence and love.

SAINT FRANCIS DE SALES

Francis was born in France in 1567. It seemed God had destined him to have a special task in the Church from his childhood. This task was to teach and write the truth about Jesus so that everyone would understand.

In school, Francis spent many years studying difficult subjects like philosophy, theology, and law. He became a lawyer, and one day heard a voice saying to him, "Leave all and follow me." So, he became a priest and went to help the poor and sinners.

Even after he became the bishop of Geneva and had many duties caring for his people, he still continued to teach.

He found time to write many books. In one, called *Introduction to the Devout Life*, he showed how people living ordinary lives can become saints.

Saint Francis Xavier, you rejoiced in all the skills and gifts God gave you. Help me to enjoy using my talents for God and to love God with all my heart.

SAINT FRANCIS XAVIER

Francis Xavier was named Patron of the Missions, and was considered the greatest missionary since Saint Paul. In Spain, as a youth, he was a great athlete, a champion runner, and the leader in his class at school. He was also a true friend to those who knew him, but was greatest at loving God.

At the University of Paris, when Francis was winning all the prizes in school, he met Ignatius Loyola. They became lifelong friends, and helped start the Society of Jesus. Ignatius once asked Francis, "What good will it do if you win all the prizes in the world, but lose your soul?"

"Send me out as a missionary," Francis replied, "and I will win the whole world for our dear Lord." Francis spent the rest of his life preaching Christ and baptizing among the peoples of India and Japan. He died in 1552.

December 3

Saint George, you understand how much courage is needed to deal with evil in life. Help me to love Christ and to be courageous like you.

SAINT GEORGE

George was a soldier and a holy man. He is often pictured in combat with a dragon. If we think of the dragon as a symbol of evil in our lives, then Saint George can be our helper whenever we have to do battle with our dragons.

George began as a soldier in the Roman Army, but rose to a high rank because of his bravery. When George became a Christian, he left the army. When the Roman Emperor published an edict persecuting Christians, George is said to have torn it down. He was martyred for his faith in Christ around the year 303.

Among the Greeks, George is called "the great martyr," and his feast is kept as a holy day in Greece.

The people of England chose him to be their patron saint. He is also the patron of Boy Scouts.

$\mathcal{S}$aint Ignatius, you read about the saints and wanted to do what they did for God. Help me to be the saint that I can be.

SAINT IGNATIUS LOYOLA

In 1521, Ignatius Loyola, the soldier, had his knee wounded in battle. While he was recovering from his wound, he began reading about Christ and the saints. "I can do what they did," he said to himself. He decided to become a "soldier of Christ."

At the University of Paris, Ignatius began to gather friends who wanted to serve with him under the banner of Christ. These young men called themselves the Companions of Jesus. People nicknamed them the Jesuits, and the order was known as the Society of Jesus.

"The Companions," Ignatius said, "are ready to do any work or go anywhere in the world for God's greater glory."

The Jesuits became famous as teachers and missionaries. They chose to live among the poor and to teach children.

ALL SAINTS DAY

Besides the saints described in this book, there are hundreds of other saints whose names are listed in the Church's canon of saints, and millions of other saints in heaven whose names are known only to God. That is why we celebrate a day for all the saints.

What does it mean to be a saint? To be proclaimed a saint by the Church has a lot of special requirements. To be a saint in God's eyes—which is more important anyway—is a lot easier. As long as you believe in Jesus and are trying to live a life that is pleasing to God and loving toward others, God says you qualify as a saint, that is, you belong to the Communion of Saints.

You are probably a saint right now. I hope you will remain among the Communion of Saints forever.

November 1